NASTY WOMEN POSTERS

WISE WORDS FROM WOMEN WHO CHANGED THE WORLD

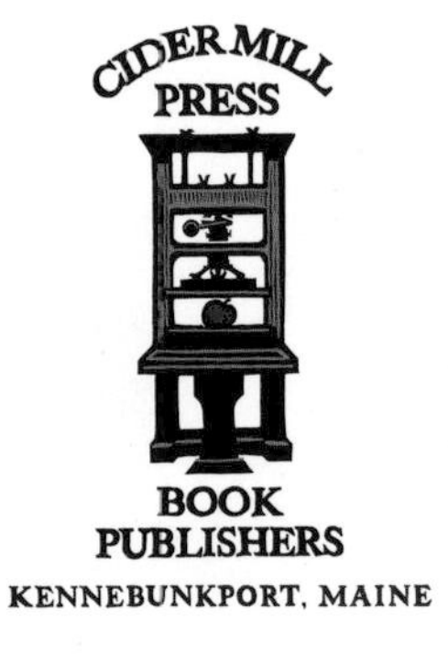

NASTY WOMEN POSTERS

13-Digit ISBN: 978-1-60433-976-5
10-Digit ISBN: 1-60433-976-4

This book may be ordered by mail from the publisher. Please include $5.99 for postage and handling. Please support your local bookseller first!

Books published by Cider Mill Press Book Publishers are available at special discounts for bulk purchases in the United States by corporations, institutions, and other organizations. For more information, please contact the publisher.

Cider Mill Press Book Publishers
"Where Good Books Are Ready for Press"
PO Box 454
12 Spring Street
Kennebunkport, Maine 04046

Visit us online! cidermillpress.com

Typography: Brothers OT, Essonnes Text, Filson Soft, Gibson, Oswald, Rockwell
Vectors on cover and posters 2, 5, 7, 8, 11, 12, 13, 19, 21, 27, 29, and 30 used under official license from Shutterstock.com.

Printed in China
1 2 3 4 5 6 7 8 9 0
First Edition

ABOUT CIDER MILL PRESS BOOK PUBLISHERS

Good ideas ripen with time. From seed to harvest, Cider Mill Press brings fine reading, information, and entertainment together between the covers of its creatively crafted books. Our Cider Mill bears fruit twice a year, publishing a new crop of titles each spring and fall.

"Where Good Books Are Ready for Press"

Visit us online at
cidermillpress.com
or write to us at
12 Spring Street
P.O. Box 454
Kennebunkport, ME 04046

WOMEN NEED NOT DEPEND ON MEN'S MEMORIES

RUTH BADER GINSBURG

"WOMEN NEED NOT DEPEND ON MEN'S MEMORIES."

–Ruth Bader Ginsburg,
in her address at the Philadelphia Bar Association quarterly meeting (October 23, 2003)

RUTH BADER GINSBURG

March 15, 1933

Known For: Gender Equality Advocacy; Women's Rights Advocacy; Reproductive Rights Advocacy; Founding Counsel Member of ACLU's Women's Rights Project (1972); Associate Justice of the United States Supreme Court (1993–Present); *United States v. Virginia* (1996)

The Notorious R.B.G., a nickname started by a creative student in reference to the rapper Notorious B.I.G., has become a touchstone figure for women's rights and the power of a dissenting voice. But Ruth Bader Ginsburg was working to secure women's rights long before she was appointed as the second female Supreme Court justice in American history and gained her larger-than-life reputation. Graduating from Columbia Law School at the top of her class, Ginsburg initially encountered difficulty in her job search, as she was not only a woman entering a male-dominated field, she was also a mother. However, she went on to become one of the strongest voices of the American judicial system.

Ginsburg's early work focused on the protections that should be afforded to women within the legal system and asserted that the practice of barring women from areas of the military and social spheres on the basis of sex should not be upheld by the law. Ginsburg is known for going against the popular grain, and her intelligent dissents have become the stuff of legend for their concision and their perspective that, while the court has made a decision, the decision is not set in stone and was not unanimous, a move that impacts future court cases on the subject. As Ginsburg has noted in various interviews, she considers a dissenter "looking out toward the future" when the decisions will be revisited, instead of focusing on when the decision has been made.

Her measured way of speaking, the candor in her dissents, and her willingness to speak out against decisions she considers incorrect or unconstitutional have garnered her popularity and respect as a member of the Supreme Court. Ginsburg is also well known for her bipartisan connections, creating friendships with many of the conservative judges on the Supreme Court, no matter their differing philosophies.

Despite multiple rounds of battling cancer, at the age of 86 Ginsburg continues to serve on the Supreme Court, making her the oldest living justice, and intends to continue representing women's rights and equality as long as she lives, proving that there is no upper limit to what women can accomplish.

YOU DON'T HAVE TO LOVE ME BUT YOU DAMN WELL HAVE TO RESPECT ME

TONI MORRISON

"YOU DON'T HAVE TO LOVE ME BUT YOU DAMN WELL HAVE TO RESPECT ME."

–Toni Morrison,
God Help the Child (2015)

TONI MORRISON

February 18, 1931 to August 5, 2019

Known For: *The Bluest Eye* (1970); *Sula* (1974); *Song of Solomon* (1977); *Paradise* (1977); *Beloved* (1987); Recipient of the Pulitzer Prize (1988); *Jazz* (1992); Recipient of the Nobel Prize for Literature (1993); Recipient of the National Arts and Humanities Award (2001); Recipient of the Presidential Medal of Freedom (2012); *God Help the Child* (2015)

One of America's most influential authors, Toni Morrison's writing focused primarily on the black experience, creating a space where she could discuss the issues facing black people in the United States as well as around the world. In an interview she gave after being awarded the Nobel Prize, Morrison said, "I stood at the border, stood at the edge and claimed it as central. Claimed it as central, and let the rest of the world move over to where I was." She worked, both as an editor and writer, to beat back the prevailing notion that stories from the perspective of black characters were inherently something on the sidelines of literary interest, instead of a topic that deserved to be in the mainstream. This is reflected multiple times throughout her career in her interviews and discussions about her writing. When one interviewer asked her why she had not considered writing from "the white perspective," Morrison pointed out that such a question would never be put to a white author.

Taking multiple years to write each of her books, Morrison's slow, methodical dedication to her craft resulted in a literary presence that will stand the test of time. Her writing deals with the spiritual, the intangible, and in many cases the incredible sense of isolation felt by her characters as they search for their identity in the face of racial prejudice. Her interpretation of culture and her personal connection to her characters breathe life into her stories.

For Morrison, writing meant truly exploring her characters' psyches, whether that meant embracing the vivid hatred of self that came with *The Bluest Eye* (1970) where a dark-skinned girl wishes she had blue eyes and paler skin, to the tormenting emotions of *Beloved* (1987), which follows an escaped slave who attempts to kill her children to save them from being brought into slavery. This dedication to her craft, the overwhelming empathy for the complex relationships that define life, and her constant representation of the struggles facing women in the world, especially black women, created a literary space for black women authors that would not exist without her contributions.

WE ARE PREPARED TO CALL

EMMA GONZÁLEZ

"WE ARE PREPARED TO CALL B.S."

–Emma González,
at an anti-gun rally in Fort Lauderdale, Florida, following the Stoneman-Douglas High School shooting (February 17, 2018)

EMMA GONZÁLEZ

November 11, 1999

Known For: March for Our Lives Movement; Gun Control Activism; Human Rights Activism

On February 14, 2018, the Stoneman-Douglas High School shooting in Parkland, Florida, became one of the largest school shootings in American history, with 17 casualties and 17 injuries. However, no one expected it to turn into a large political and social movement. Student survivors took their experiences to social media and spoke out about the shooting to media outlets, decrying any attempts to downplay the shooter's involvement and protesting the representation of school shootings in American media and politics. Unlike previous school shootings, the Stoneman-Douglas High School students did not allow the media to shape the narrative. Instead, they stepped up and spoke out against organizations like the National Rifle Association, which has donated large sums to politicians who in turn underrepresent the impact of gun violence in the United States. This started a trend on Twitter and other media outlets of protestors commenting on politicians' sympathetic statuses with the donations they received from the NRA.

One student to emerge from this outcry was Emma González. Known for her distinctive shaved head and empowering language, González spoke at a press conference just days after the shooting, issuing her now iconic "We call B.S." line that struck the nation. In the following months, students around the world organized protests under the banner of March for Our Lives, mobilizing survivors to stand up against the senseless violence and march on Washington, D.C. to protest the administration's remarks and drive home their message: "Never again."

Enduring constant slander by conservative news outlets, including photoshopped images showing her tearing the American Constitution in half, and accusations by national political figures that she was a crisis actor, González refused to back down, repeating her call to tighten both public and private gun sale regulations across all states. Working closely with other survivors of the school shooting, González not only helped create the March for Our Lives movement, she also continues to speak out about her PTSD and daily struggles in the aftermath of the shooting, helping destigmatize the topic for other survivors of gun violence.

During the March for Our Lives event in Washington, D.C., González spoke about the students who had been killed during the shooting, listing the milestones in their lives they would not be able to accomplish. Her speech was followed by a poignant moment of silence, concluding at 6 minutes and 20 seconds, the exact amount of time the shooter was loose in the halls of the school before blending in with students evacuating and evading capture for an hour. She ended her speech with a call to "Fight for your lives before it's someone else's job." This powerful outcry solidified the actions of the movement, which rallied 880 similar events across the world. With over 2 million attendees nationwide, the March was one of the largest protests in American history, outlining the power of students to change public perception.

González has quickly become a role model for younger generations, proving that anyone can make a meaningful impact. Her speeches and arguments continue to be empowering and passionate, refusing to follow the polite structure of political debate that has become prevalent in today's culture, and her insistence that political figures be held accountable for their actions and no longer allowed to curtail the truth engendered a larger societal push for accountability in both the political sphere and in the media.

NO MATTER WHAT YOUR FIGHT, DON'T BE LADYLIKE!

MARY HARRIS JONES

"NO MATTER WHAT YOUR FIGHT, DON'T BE LADYLIKE!"

–Mary Harris Jones,
The Autobiography of Mother Jones (1925)

MARY HARRIS JONES

c. 1837 to November 30, 1930

Known For: Labor Activism; Union Activism; Economic Justice Activism; The Great Railroad Strike of 1877; Haymarket Day Demonstration (1886)

Mary Harris Jones, better known as Mother Jones, earned her matronly nickname from her motherly treatment of miners during the Great Railroad Strike of 1877, though her personality was anything but demure. She did not define herself as an activist, but rather took on her own name: "hell-raiser." While she herself did not support women's suffrage, stating, "You don't need a vote to raise hell," Jones railed against the treatment of workers across the United States, speaking out on behalf of laborers and pushing for a shorter workweek and shorter workdays, as well as improvement of working conditions. She partnered with unions and organized strikers to protest the inequality between business owners and their employees, urging them to use the power of collective bargaining to cement their own positions in the business. On top of looking to improve the conditions for the adult working class, she also worked to abolish child labor, leading a children's march from Philadelphia through New York City, ending at President Theodore Roosevelt's Long Island home.

Jones was known for her oratory skills, and her speeches contained the language of the working class, as well as a tenacity that terrified those who were against unions. She traveled across the country, taking up the cause of strikes and protests along the way, gaining herself a reputation as a folk hero and becoming one of the most recognizable leaders of the movement. She also condemned the white supremacism found in many corners of the union movement, and worked for inclusion of African American, Mexican, and Italian workers, arguing they were the true foundation of the cause.

Jones serves as an inspiration to modern-day labor movements and has once again risen to popularity in the face of greater economic disparity and anti-union movements being pushed by large corporations. She stands as a reminder for anyone looking to create change in their community that they should be ready to raise hell.

WE MUST ALWAYS ATTEMPT TO LIFT AS WE CLIMB

ANGELA DAVIS

"WE MUST ALWAYS ATTEMPT TO LIFT AS WE CLIMB."

–Angela Davis,
Women, Culture & Politics (1989)

ANGELA DAVIS

Born January 26, 1944

Known For: Black Rights Activism; Women's Rights Activism; Black Panther Involvement; Communist Party Involvement; Marin County Courthouse Incident (1970); *If They Come in the Morning* (1971); *Women, Race & Class* (1981); *Women, Culture & Politics* (1989); *Are Prisons Obsolete?* (2003); *Freedom is a Constant Struggle* (2015)

Angela Yvonne Davis became known through her role in the counterculture of the 1960s and '70s, although she has mentioned she feels that later generations recognize her only as "a hairdo." While her iconic afro caused her to stand out from the crowd, her fierce intelligence and dedication to black rights, women's rights, human rights, and her cry for prison reformation, are what set her apart.

Born in segregated Birmingham, Alabama, Davis was familiar with racial tensions from a young age, detailing her memories of the racial violence prevalent in her neighborhood, from the white police officers who frequently stopped her on the street under the assumption she was a militant because of her natural hair, to the 16th Street Baptist Church Bombing in 1963, noting in one interview that she knew many of the girls present at the church at that time. In an interview on the violent actions of different revolutionary groups, Davis outlined the "hidden" violence of the status quo, noting that for oppressed minorities up against systemic inequality, violence may be their only option to protect themselves and their families.

Davis was a member of The Black Panthers, as well as the American Communist Party, the latter bringing her duress in her position as a professor at the University of California, Los Angeles. As she boasted in one panel held at the college in 2019, "I got fired twice." While the board first attempted to fire her for her association with the American Communist Party in 1969, it was deemed she could not be fired because of her political associations, and she was reinstated, only to be fired a second time in 1970 due to her vehement opposition to the treatment of the People's Park demonstrators in Berkeley. Despite the outcry from the American Association of University Professors at her treatment, Davis did not lecture again at UCLA until 45 years later. This did not slow Davis's passion for education, however; she went on to teach at San Francisco State University, University of California, Santa Cruz, and Rutgers University, as well as countless other universities, focusing on ethics and feminist studies.

Later in her divisive life, Davis was incarcerated following her association with (and the resulting escape attempt during the trial of) George Jackson, one of the inmates and Black Panther members charged with killing a prison guard at Soledad Prison. However, during her imprisonment, Davis continued to speak out against racism and the use of the prison system to oppress minorities. Throughout her efforts to regain her freedom, one facet of her commitment to helping others was the rebranding of the campaign as not just an effort to free Davis, but to also free all political prisoners held unjustly. After a lengthy campaign, Davis was given the verdict of not guilty by an all-white jury and finally released in 1972. Not content with just her freedom, Davis continues to protest the use of the American penal system, striving to lift others up to join her in freedom.

THE ONLY INTERESTING IDEAS ARE HERESIES

SUSAN SONTAG

"THE ONLY INTERESTING IDEAS ARE HERESIES."

–Susan Sontag,
in her journal (June 30, 1975, Paris)

SUSAN SONTAG

January 16, 1933 to December 28, 2004

Known For: Human Rights Activism; *The Benefactor* (1963); *Notes on "Camp"* (1964); *Against Interpretation* (1966); *On Photography* (1977); *Illness As Metaphor* (1978); *AIDS and Its Metaphors* (1989); Commandeur de l'Ordre des Arts et des Lettres (1999); *America* (1999); *Regarding the Pain of Others* (2003)

Through her writing and public persona, Susan Sontag championed a kind of distance and disinterest that belied the insightful content of her creations. Fascinated with the philosophical interpretation of many aspects of culture, Sontag gained notoriety for her work *Notes on "Camp"* (1964), in which she discussed taste and style in the gay community. In many ways, Sontag rejected the traditional expectations of a female writer, keeping her personal life largely private, and writing against the idea of revering women's beauty as separate from their intelligence and internal life. Her writings can be seen as an ever-evolving conversation about the complexities of human life, and she takes a critical look at the idea of experience and interpretation, and how the norms of criticism cannot ultimately describe a work. Not only an author, Sontag wrote screenplays, and had a fascination with European films that reached its height during her time in Paris.

Sontag was not one to shy away from giving her opinion on a wide range of different subjects, and was known for championing freedom of expression for authors on an international scale through her work as president of PEN America from 1987 to 1989. Sontag was one of the many protestors who spoke out against the United States' involvement in the Vietnam War, yet she was unafraid to admit she had grown from previous statements. In many cases, Sontag would critique her past works, even going so far as to decry her involvement in the Communist Party during her youth, instead favoring a more liberal standpoint. By allowing herself to develop and change throughout her time in the spotlight, as well as in her writing, Sontag in turn facilitated her own growth and the growth of her audience. From her work supporting her friend with AIDS to the end of his life to her investigation of the stigma surrounding the AIDS crisis in her work *AIDS and Its Metaphors* (1989), Sontag cultivated a duality and complexity in her work that outlined her incredible talent as a writer and her own journey of maturity, establishing her as one of the greatest writers of her time.

ONE IS NOT BORN, BUT RATHER BECOMES A WOMAN

SIMONE DE BEAUVOIR

"ONE IS NOT BORN, BUT RATHER BECOMES A WOMAN."

–Simone de Beauvoir,
The Second Sex (*Le Deuxième Sexe*, 1949)

SIMONE DE BEAUVOIR

January 8, 1908 to April 14, 1986

Known For: Advancement of Feminist Theory; Feminist Movement; Existentialism and Existential Ethics; Women's Rights Activism; Reproductive Rights Activism; Editor of *Modern Times* (*Les Temps Modernes*) (1945–1986); *The Second Sex* (*Le Deuxième Sexe*) (1949); "Manifesto of the 343 (Manifeste des 343)" (1971)

When Simone de Beauvoir published *The Second Sex* in 1949, the concept that women were considered second-class citizens had not been discussed in writing before. A true pioneer of the feminist movement, de Beauvoir's book dealt with the unequal distribution of housework in the average household and the pressures placed on women to tend to their children and rely entirely on their husbands to support them. De Beauvoir also explored the idea of sex being separate from gender, a modern concept that was largely unheard of at the time. Her work gained rampant attention throughout the United States after it was translated and has become the cornerstone text for many aspects of the feminist movement. However, her life's work did not just deal with the issues of women's rights. She also worked to expand the study of human sexuality and was open about her own relationship to Jean-Paul Sartre (as well as other lovers) in an effort to destigmatize public perceptions about relationships and physical intimacy.

De Beauvoir drew attention to the conditioning placed on women from a young age to be submissive and ashamed of themselves and their bodies, illustrating in her *Questionnaire* interview in 1975 the different ways boys and girls are raised, as boys are often encouraged to be aggressive and independent, while girls are often raised to be complacent and cautious. She was one of the first people to bring awareness to the fact that the concept of womanhood as it has been construed throughout history is an incredibly subjective topic, one that depends on social pressures and the culture of the time to survive. Throughout her life, she worked to increase the freedoms allowed to women of all age groups and socio-economic backgrounds, and spoke up to end the taboo surrounding abortion with her work on the "Manifesto of the 343" in 1971, which included the testimonies of women who had received illegal abortions in France at the time. Through her research into the systematic oppression facing women all over the world, her work championing the cause of equality, and her objective assessment of the concepts of gender and sexuality, de Beauvoir helped advance the cause of women's liberation and freedom of sexual expression by leaps and bounds, and her writing continues to encourage modern women to speak out against their own oppression and continue the steady dismantling of restrictive societal norms.

I AM A STAR AS WELL AS A WOMAN, AND THEY HAVE TO DEAL WITH THE TWO

NINA SIMONE

"I AM A STAR AS WELL AS A WOMAN, AND THEY HAVE TO DEAL WITH THE TWO."

–Nina Simone,
in an interview with Tim Sebastian on BBC *HARDtalk* (1999)

NINA SIMONE

February 21, 1933 to April 21, 2003

Known For: Black Empowerment; Civil Rights Activism; Singer of the Black Revolution; Political Protest Songs; "Mississippi Goddam" (1964); "Why? (The King of Love Is Dead)" (1968); "To Be Young, Gifted and Black" (1969); *I Put a Spell On You* (1993); Grammy Hall of Fame Award (2000)

Born Eunice Waymon, Nina Simone chose her stage name in 1954 based on the nickname "niña," given to her by a boyfriend, and "Simone" after actress Simone Signoret. While Simone's original aspirations included becoming a classical pianist, due to financial troubles and racial prejudice, she was unable to continue her piano education, and instead turned to singing in order to make extra money. Starting her singing career performing at bars, Simone was offered a record deal by Bethlehem Records, and in 1958 recorded her version of the song "I Loves You, Porgy" from the 1935 English-language opera "Porgy & Bess." Her musical style combined blues and jazz with classical themes and inspired piano riffs, and her choice of music ran the gambit from children's songs to protest anthems, securing her reputation as a genre-defying artist. But it wasn't until the assassination of Civil Rights activist Medgar Evers and the 16th Street Baptist Church Bombing in Birmingham, Alabama, in 1963 that Simone decided to fuse her commitment to the Civil Rights Movement with her musical talent, producing her original song "Mississippi Goddam" in 1964. The song was banned in the Southern United States for its message, but this did not stop Simone's involvement in the Civil Rights Movement. She would go on to write several protest anthems, including "To Be Young, Gifted and Black" after a quote by her friend, writer Lorraine Hansberry, who died from cancer in 1965 at the age of 34.

As Simone's musical popularity continued to climb, her songs covered topics like the Eurocentric beauty standards forced onto black women in the 1966 song "Four Women." She noted in her autobiography *I Put a Spell On You* (1993) that she wrote this song in hopes that women of color would accept their natural beauty instead of trying to change themselves into something they were not. Simone would eventually move out of the United States (a choice she attributed to the racism prevalent in the country at the time) but would continue to find popularity on the international scene. While Simone was known for her particular demands when it came to her performances, she would make a point to visit with other black artists and activists while on tour, asserting in one interview released by her estate in 2013 that any little difference she could make in their lives was worth her time, no matter how tired she was after performing.

THE ONLY TIRED I WAS WAS TIRED OF GIVING IN

ROSA PARKS

"THE ONLY TIRED I WAS, WAS TIRED OF GIVING IN."

–***Rosa Parks,***
Rosa Parks: My Story (1992)

ROSA PARKS

February 4, 1913 to October 24, 2005

Known For: Civil Rights Activism; Anti-Segregation Activism; Secretary of the Montgomery Chapter of the National Association for the Advancement of Colored People (NAACP) (1943–c. 1990s); Montgomery Bus Boycott (1955–1956); Detroit Civil Rights Movement (1963); *Rosa Parks: My Story* (1992); Recipient of the Presidential Medal of Honor (1996); Recipient of the Congressional Gold Medal (1999)

Rosa Parks was not the first person to refuse to give up their seat on a segregated bus, but her story has become synonymous with the Civil Rights Movement and how small acts of rebellion can become the foundation of a larger push for change. Born in Tuskegee, Alabama, Parks grew up in highly segregated areas of the Southern United States, and was frequently the subject of discrimination, as well as witness to racial violence. When she boarded a segregated bus in Montgomery, Alabama, on December 1, 1955, Parks was not the exhausted worker the media would later portray her as, noting in her autobiography *Rosa Parks: My Story* (1992) that she "was not tired physically," and that the only tired she was "was tired of giving in." When pressured by a white passenger to give up her seat, a practice that was expected in segregated areas of the South, Parks refused and was arrested. Not only did her act of resistance bring attention to the Civil Rights Movement and help start the Montgomery Bus Boycott, it soon became the iconic act of resistance in the battle against segregated transportation.

Parks's fight against segregation did not come without a cost, and she was fired from her job, as well as sent death threats for her involvement with the movement. Still, she continued to fight for civil rights, participating in countless other marches throughout the '60s, and became notable for her involvement in the Detroit Civil Rights Movement. Not only a champion for civil rights, Parks also spoke out in support of political prisoners, and continued to champion the cause of equality through the rest of her life. Her effect on the Civil Rights Movement, as well as the inspiration she provides for other activists, has solidified her place in the halls of great women, and she continues to motivate generations of activists to speak out against the injustices of their society and work for change, both large and small.

THE BROTHER THAT GETS ME IS GOING TO GET ONE HELL OF A FABULOUS WOMAN

ARETHA FRANKLIN

"THE BROTHER THAT GETS ME IS GOING TO GET ONE HELL OF A FABULOUS WOMAN."

–Aretha Franklin,
"Aretha Franklin: Soul of the Queen" (*Vanity Fair*, March 1, 1994)

ARETHA FRANKLIN

March 25, 1942 to August 16, 2018

Known For: The Queen of Soul; Civil Rights Movement; Women's Rights; Indigenous Peoples Activism and Support; "Respect" (1967); First Woman Inducted into Rock and Roll Hall of Fame (1987); Recipient of the Grammy Lifetime Achievement Award (1994); Recipient of the Presidential Medal of Freedom (2005)

The Queen of Soul, Aretha Franklin has become a household name across America. Long before Beyoncé and Madonna stepped into the limelight, Aretha was one of the first modern musicians to be known only by their first name. Her music is invigorating, combining her smoky, bluesy, gospel-choir shaped voice with soul and sass. Her voice became synonymous with the fight for Civil Rights and female equality, the demanding lyrics of "Respect" the anthem for anyone facing oppression. While Aretha said that she never intended "Respect" to become a women's rights song, she noted "I don't make it a practice to put my politics into my music or social commentary. But the fact that 'Respect' naturally became a battle cry and anthem for a nation shows me something."

While much of the discussion about Aretha centers around her incredible musical talents, her actions in the activism sphere are far from insignificant. Friends with Martin Luther King Jr. during the Civil Rights Movement, Aretha weighed in heavily on the effort, stipulating in her contract that she would never play at segregated venues and supporting King and his family closely during the height of the movement. After King's assassination, Aretha performed at his funeral, and she continued to support King's wife, Coretta Scott King, in her leadership of the movement.

Like many women who find themselves in the spotlight, Aretha has been cast in various lights by the media, from the shy, insecure, depressed soul singer to the booming diva who calls off shows at a moment's notice and gets what she wants when she wants it, no exceptions. Her personality is as multifaceted as her music, and her personal struggles with depression, alcoholism, and insecurity, as well as a tumultuous family life, have become an inspiration to countless fans over the years. But even though her fans identify with her complex inner life, Aretha held the press at arm's length, allowing them to devour her famed feuds with other artists but keeping her personal life as private as possible, especially following their incessant attempts to dig deeper into her tumultuous marriage to Ted White.

While for some artists "diva" is an insult, Aretha wore the title as a badge of pride, willing to rerecord tracks at the drop of a hat if she felt her part was underrepresented and breaking connections with several labels that she felt misrepresented her interests. While society tends to portray women who know what they want as pushy or overbearing, Aretha wielded her forceful personality regardless of what anyone thought about her, using her position as a recognizable star to bring attention to global and local issues. Awarded the Grammy Lifetime Achievement Award in 1994 and the Presidential Medal of Freedom in 2005, Aretha was a woman well aware of her own value and was determined no one would shoot her down, defining herself as a fabulous woman worthy of respect.

YOU DON'T HAVE TO BE ANYTHING BUT YOURSELF TO BE WORTHY

TARANA BURKE

"YOU DON'T HAVE TO BE ANYTHING BUT YOURSELF TO BE WORTHY."

–Tarana Burke,
in her discussion at Hofstra University
(November 1, 2017)

TARANA BURKE

September 12, 1973

Known For: #MeToo Movement; Women's Rights Activism; Civil Rights Activism; Founder of Just Be Inc. (2006); Senior Director of Girls for Gender Equity in Brooklyn (2018–Present); Recipient of the Voice of the Year (VOTY) Catalyst Award from SheKnows Media (2018)

While #MeToo started trending across the internet in 2017, just two days after the *New York Times* investigated the sexual harassment claims against Harvey Weinstein, a Hollywood film producer, the movement began much earlier. Tarana Burke started her career working to end racial discrimination and housing inequality, and supporting economic justice. However, upon moving to Selma, Alabama, Burke encountered countless black girls who had experienced sexual assault and other forms of abuse without any form of support. She herself a survivor of sexual violence at a young age, Burke founded Just Be Inc. to empower and support black girls.

The phrase "me too" was coined by Burke after an interaction with a girl at a summer camp who approached Burke about the girl's own sexual assault. Burke wrote on the website for Just Be Inc. that "I couldn't even bring myself to whisper... me too" in response to the girl's testimony. Burke has since offered the phrase "Me too" as a way of assuring these survivors that they are not alone, that there are people there to help and support them through their healing. The sudden popularity of the #MeToo movement was propelled by Alyssa Milano, an American actress and activist who tweeted a call for other people to respond to her tweet with the phrase "Me too" if they had ever been sexually harassed or assaulted. Beginning on October 15, 2017, the tweet garnered over 50,000 responses, and the overwhelming swell of solidarity behind the movement crossed over to other social media platforms, with over 12 million posts and comments worldwide.

Burke has since been credited with helping break down the stigma surrounding survivors of sexual assault speaking about their experience, and her openness about the topic has inspired other survivors to come forward, leading off a chain reaction within the media where many prominent figures were convicted of sexual assault, including well-known actor Bill Cosby in 2018. While Burke has spoken out against the "assumed guilty" convictions and firing of other individuals accused of sexual assault egged on by the media, she strives to provide survivors with the confidence to tell their stories, seek justice and healing, and bring awareness to the need to end the taboo surrounding discussing sexual assault for both survivors and advocates.

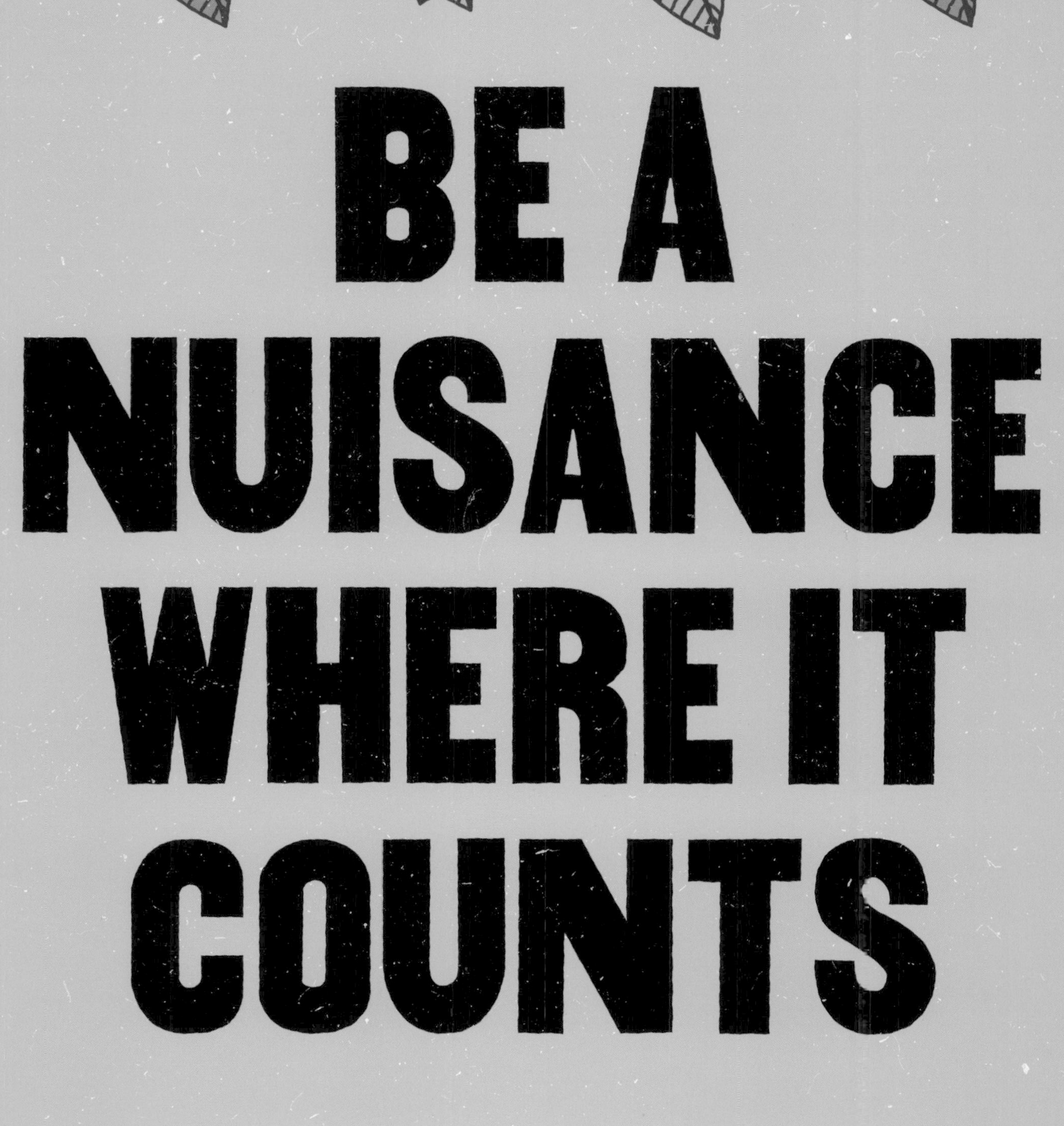
BE A
NUISANCE
WHERE IT
COUNTS
MARJORY STONEMAN DOUGLAS

"BE A NUISANCE WHERE IT COUNTS."

–Marjory Stoneman Douglas,
The Everglades (1947)

MARJORY STONEMAN DOUGLAS

April 7, 1890 to May 14, 1998

Known For: Women's Rights Activism; Environmental Activism; *The Everglades: River of Grass* (1947); Florida Everglades Conservation; Campaign to Create Everglades National Park

Marjory Stoneman Douglas is an incredible example of how activism isn't just for the younger generation. Beginning her support of women's rights, racial justice, and conservation through her column "The Galley" in the *Miami Herald*, Stoneman never identified herself as feminist, but she strove for women's independence and participated in the women's suffrage movement during her college years. However, her most notable work, the protection of the Florida Everglades, did not take place until much later in her life with the publication of *The Everglades: River of Grass* in 1947, the same year Everglades National Parks was established. While she had been an advocate for the creation of the park for many years before its founding, her tireless work to protect the Everglades from unnecessary development took on a new life during the late '40s and '50s. She spoke out against the canal and dam systems being created in the Everglades to try and protect agriculture zones from flooding, noting that this interrupted the area's ecological balance and would destroy the wetlands. In 1970, at the age of 79, she formed Friends of the Everglades to popularize support for the natural landscape and heighten awareness about how the complexity of nature can be trampled by human intervention. Thanks to her involvement as well as contributions from Friends of the Everglades, she helped to prevent large-scale damage to the Everglades despite population growth in South Florida and a push to drain the wetlands for use as farmland.

Not only did Douglas help stave off several construction projects in the area, including a proposed jetport, her advocacy acted as a model for other grassroots protest movements that would strive to protect unblemished wilderness from destruction and exploitation all over the world. Her work gained worldwide recognition and in 1993 she was awarded the Presidential Medal of Freedom. Douglas continued to advocate for environmental protection and conservation throughout her entire life, living to the ripe age of 108. Her house and property are now managed by the Florida Park Service as a memorial to her tireless protection of the Everglades and her incredible resilience and dedication to preserving the environment.

WOMEN MUST TRY TO DO THINGS AS MEN HAVE TRIED. WHEN THEY FAIL, THEIR FAILURE MUST BE A CHALLENGE TO OTHERS.

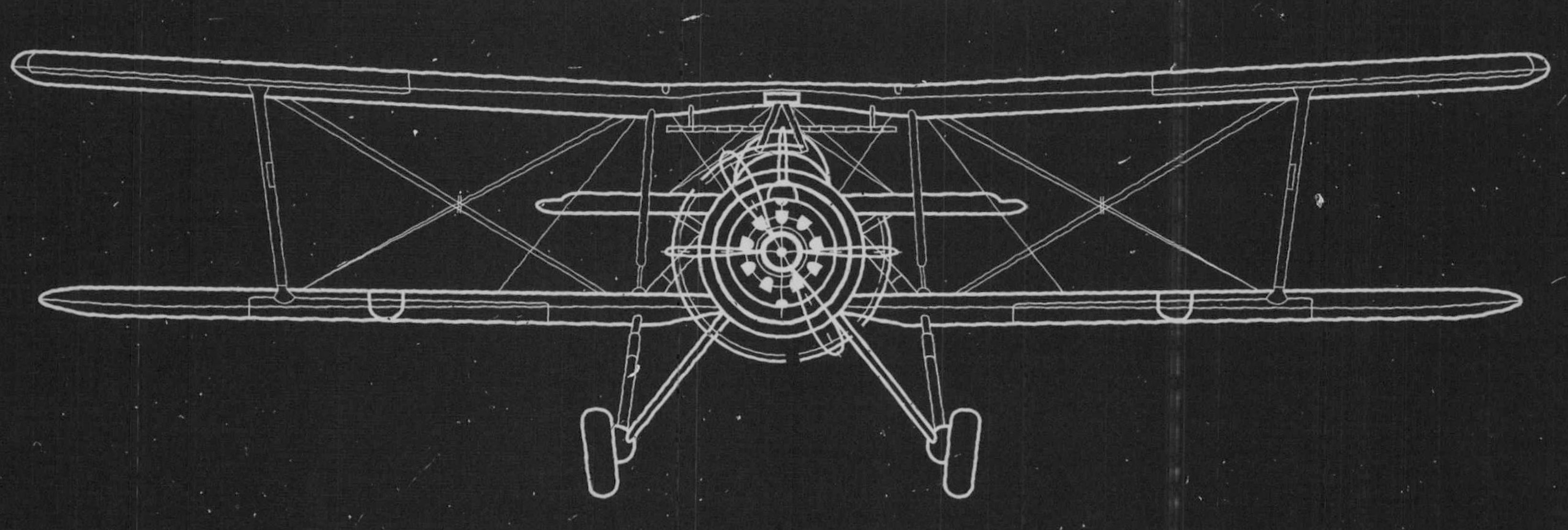

AMELIA EARHART

"WOMEN MUST TRY TO DO THINGS AS MEN HAVE TRIED. WHEN THEY FAIL, THEIR FAILURE MUST BE A CHALLENGE TO OTHERS."

–Amelia Earhart,
in her last letter to her husband George P. Putnam
before her final flight (*Last Flight*, 1937)

AMELIA EARHART

(1897–1937)

Known For: Co-Founder of The Ninety-Nine (1929); First Female Solo Transatlantic Flight (1932); Women's Rights Advocate; Attempting to Circumnavigate the Globe by Plane (1937)

Born in Atchison, Kansas, Amelia Earhart has become the quintessential symbol of exploration and discovery, and for good reason. Almost everyone knows her as the first woman to fly solo across the Atlantic Ocean in 1932, and her disappearance while attempting to circumnavigate the globe in 1937. But there is more to the story of Amelia Earhart than her mysterious disappearance.

After her first airplane ride in 1920, Earhart recalled, "As soon as we left the ground, I knew I myself had to fly." Working under the instruction of another female aviation pioneer, Anita "Neta" Snook, Earhart was a quick study and gained her pilot's license just a few years later. Earhart purchased her first plane in 1921, and in 1922 became the first woman to fly solo above 14,000 feet. While Earhart was a local phenomenon during the early '20s, her true rise to fame did not take place until 1928, when she was selected to be the first woman to fly across the Atlantic Ocean. After the successful flight, Earhart was met with wild acclaim, yet she simply described herself to the press as "a sack of potatoes" on the flight, as she was not the pilot.

The nickname "Lady Lindy" was a reference to Charles A. Lindbergh, the first man to complete a solo transatlantic flight in 1927, but Earhart's accomplishments never took the backseat to any man, including her husband. In her prenuptial agreement with George P. Putnam, Earhart specified that, "I shall not hold you to any medieval code of faithfulness to me nor shall I consider myself bound to you similarly...Please let us not interfere with the other's work or play." She also noted that, "I cannot guarantee to endure at all the confinements of even an attractive cage," with the caveat that Putnam would promise to let her "go in a year if we find no happiness together." Earhart's tenacity and independence were undeniable, and at one point she went as far as to call out the *New York Times* publicly for incorrectly addressing her by using her husband's last name.

Ironically, Putnam is the one who arranged for Earhart's largely autobiographical *Last Flight* to be published in 1937. She had been working on the book before her flight but was unable to finish it due to her disappearance. Putnam, working as joint editor and publisher, noted Earhart had given him a letter to read in case her monumental flight was to be her last, finishing *Last Flight* with Earhart's iconic assurance: "Women must try to do things as men have tried. When they fail, their failure must be a challenge to others." Even from beyond the unknown, Earhart challenged women everywhere to see her failure not as a defeat, but as a chance for the next woman to demonstrate that she could do anything she wanted.

WE'LL HAVE OUR
RIGHTS;
SEE IF WE DON'T;
AND YOU CAN'T
STOP US
FROM THEM;
SEE IF YOU CAN.

SOJOURNER TRUTH

"WE'LL HAVE OUR RIGHTS; SEE IF WE DON'T; AND YOU CAN'T STOP US FROM THEM; SEE IF YOU CAN."

–Sojourner Truth,
in a speech on women's rights at the Mob Convention
in New York (September 8, 1853)

SOJOURNER TRUTH

c. 1797 to November 26, 1883

Known For: Abolitionism; Human Rights Activism; Women's Suffrage; Women's Rights Activism; Equal Rights Movement; *The Narrative of Sojourner Truth: A Northern Slave* (1850); "Ain't I a Woman?" (1851)

One of the most recognizable abolitionists of her time, Isabella Baumfree changed her name to Sojourner Truth in her 40s when she worked as a minister's assistant. For Truth, slavery was more than just a morally corrupt institution: it was part of her history. Born into slavery in upstate New York where nearly all of her siblings were sold away, Truth was sold a total of four times. Truth eventually escaped slavery with her daughter Sophie and soon rescued her son Peter, who was illegally sold to Alabama. To gain her freedom she had to leave behind her husband Thomas and her remaining children. After gaining her freedom, Truth continued to fight for the cause of abolition and women's rights and worked with prominent abolitionists including Frederick Douglass and William Lloyd Garrison.

One of her most famous speeches has come to be known as "Ain't I a Woman?" and was given at a women's rights conference in Akron, Ohio, in 1851. Although the first record of her speech did not include the now-famous phrase "Ain't I a woman?", Truth's simple but powerful way of speaking carries through to the listener. In it, she outlines that she had felt the pain and struggles of being a woman, that her race did not make her less of a woman, and that there should be no discrimination against women when it comes to civil rights. She attacked the idea that women were lower than men because Christ was a man, stating: "Where did your Christ come from? From God and a woman! Man had nothing to do with Him." She also spoke against the assumption that women were less intelligent than men and because of that deserved less civil rights, insisting that everyone should have rights, regardless of their intellect.

Truth gained a reputation as an honest, powerful public speaker who spoke at numerous rallies, and helped garner support for the Union army during the American Civil War, as well as organizing supplies for black soldiers. Even near the end of her life, Truth continued to fight back against segregation and oppression, winning a lawsuit against a streetcar conductor who tried to bar her from entering the vehicle in the mid-1860s. Her tenacity and steadfastness in the face of discrimination helped transform the United States and paved the way for the Civil Rights Movement that was to come; she also laid the groundwork for true universal suffrage, which would not come about until over 80 years after her death.

WE CAN'T SAVE THE WORLD BY PLAYING BY THE RULES, BECAUSE THE RULES HAVE TO BE CHANGED.

GRETA THUNBERG

"WE CAN'T SAVE THE WORLD BY PLAYING BY THE RULES, BECAUSE THE RULES HAVE TO BE CHANGED."

–Greta Thunberg,
in her Declaration of Rebellion at the Extinction Rebellion
in Parliament Square, London (October 31, 2018)

GRETA THUNBERG

January 3, 2003

Known For: School Strike for Climate (Skolstrejk för klimatet) (2018); Zero-Carbon Lifestyle; Environmental Activism; Climate Change Activism; Recipient of Person of the Year from *Time* magazine (2019)

At just 16 years old, Greta Thunberg has become an important player in the discussion about climate change. At the age of 8, she became aware of the climate crisis, and after falling into a severe depression was diagnosed with Asperger syndrome, OCD, and selective mutism. In interviews she refers to her diagnosis with Asperger syndrome as "her superpower," as it allows her to see the issue of climate change more clearly. After convincing her family to switch to a carbon-neutral lifestyle by going vegan and avoiding air travel, Thunberg gained popularity by striking at the Swedish parliament and organizing Fridays for Future, a series of school strikes to bring awareness to the climate crisis. Not one to sacrifice her carbon-neutral lifestyle for international awareness, Thunberg sailed across the Atlantic Ocean in 2019, maintaining a zero-carbon impact throughout the trip and illustrating her dedication to preventing climate change on both a personal and global level.

Inspired by the actions of Stoneman-Douglas School Shooting survivors like Emma González (see page 8) and their March for Our Lives protest, Thunberg has spoken up for the role of youth in political activism while still calling on the older generations to reform their use of environmental resources. Like many activists her age, Thunberg has been subject to criticism from media outlets and climate change deniers, with accusations ranging from implying she has her papers written for her, to President Donald Trump dismissing her speech calling for immediate action on climate change, sarcastically stating, "She seems like a very happy young girl looking forward to a bright and wonderful future. So nice to see!" Thunberg retaliated by making this belittling tweet her profile bio on Twitter and continues to stand up to those who seek to discredit her because she is young or who attempt to use her neurodivergence against her.

Thunberg is direct and to the point. In her November 2018 TED Talk, Thunberg noted that she has no use for social language that dances around an issue. Unlike many environmental activists, she does not subscribe to the overarching message of hope in her presentations, as she believes it is more important to confront the dire realities of the climate crisis. Thunberg herself has noted she sees things "in black and white" due to her diagnosis with Asperger's, but she also notes that human survival must be "in shades of gray" if there is to be a future for her generation. By refusing to use placatory language and emphasizing the crisis facing the world, her words have reached a larger audience and reflect the panic felt by younger generations.

By not backing down when faced with criticism and continually presenting facts in the face of deniers, Thunberg continues the trend of modern-day activists by representing truth openly in the face of political and social figures who try and bury it in order to push their own agendas.

TO FREE US FROM THE EXPECTATIONS OF OTHERS, TO GIVE US BACK TO OURSELVES—THERE LIES THE GREAT, SINGULAR POWER OF SELF-RESPECT.

JOAN DIDION

"TO FREE US FROM THE EXPECTATIONS OF OTHERS, TO GIVE US BACK TO OURSELVES—THERE LIES THE GREAT, SINGULAR POWER OF SELF-RESPECT."

–Joan Didion,
"On Self-Respect" (*Vogue*, 1961)

JOAN DIDION

December 5, 1934

Known For: Essayist and Screenwriter; Participant in "New Journalism" Movement; *Run River* (1963); *Slouching Towards Bethlehem* (1968); *Play It as It Lays* (1970); *Panic in Needle Park* (1971); *A Star is Born* (1981); *Up Close and Personal* (1996); *Political Fictions* (2001); Recipient of the American Academy of Arts & Letters Gold Medal in Criticism and Belles Letters (2005); Recipient of the National Medal of Arts and Humanities (2013)

Joan Didion was a shy, quiet child who loved to read. She pushed herself to overcome her shyness from a young age by participating in activities like theater and public speaking. She attended the University of California, Berkeley and shortly before leaving the university she won a *Vogue* magazine essay contest, which landed her a job working for *Vogue* in New York. During the next two years, Didion became a contributing writer, and also worked on her own writing on the side. She wrote her first novel *Run River* in 1963 while on staff at the magazine.

After two years working in New York, Didion married John Gregory Dunne and moved to Los Angeles, where she began writing essays that centered around the California counterculture. Her essay "Slouching Towards Bethlehem" gained favorable attention when it was published in *The Saturday Evening Post* in 1967. The essay became an iconic depiction of the social and political turmoil of the time. The following year, a collection of Didion's essays was published under the same title about life in California in the 1960s. Didion's writing is considered part of the "New Journalism" movement in which writers such as Tom Wolfe, Truman Capote, and Norman Mailer developed a mode of nonfiction writing that went outside the bounds of traditional investigative journalism by virtue of writers fully immersing themselves in the story and employing characteristics more indicative of fiction writing such as strong character development and plot building.

Didion also took an interest in the film industry and, together with her husband, went on to write a number of screenplays including *Panic in Needle Park* (1971) and *A Star is Born* (1981). In the early 2000s Didion lost both her husband and daughter to separate illnesses. Despite her losses, she continued to turn to writing as a way to observe and make sense of her world. Didion has and continues to use her talent for writing and storytelling to make important and timely commentaries on the inner workings of Hollywood, social justice, foreign affairs, and life and culture in America.

WHEREVER WE ARE, THERE IS SOMETHING IN OUR LIVES THAT WE CAN DO, NO MATTER HOW SMALL IT IS.

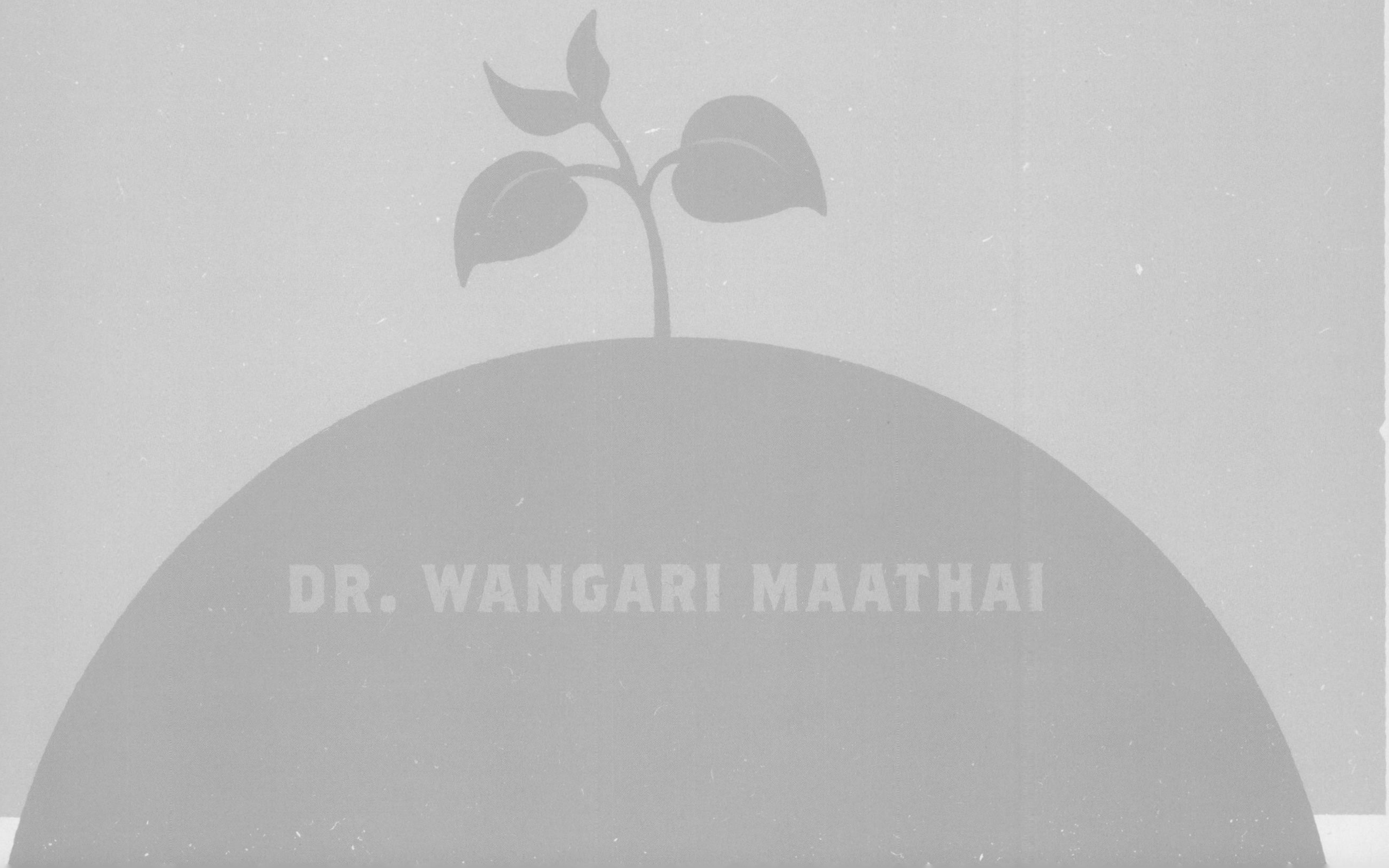

DR. WANGARI MAATHAI

"WHEREVER WE ARE, THERE IS SOMETHING IN OUR LIVES THAT WE CAN DO, NO MATTER HOW SMALL IT IS."

–Dr. Wangari Maathai,
in her address at the Botanic Gardens Conservation International
20th Anniversary Celebration (February 2007)

DR. WANGARI MAATHAI

April 1, 1940 to September 25, 2011

Known For: The Green Belt Movement; Environmental Activism; Global Climate Change Activism; Political Activism; Women's Rights Activism; Kenyan Assistant Minister for Environment, Natural Resources, and Wildlife (2002); Recipient of the Nobel Peace Prize (2004)

Those who think of environmental activism as largely a Western movement are not only doing the rest of the world a great disservice, they are ignoring contributions from impactful women like Dr. Wangari Maathai. Founder of the Green Belt Movement, a group that focuses on community-led reforestation efforts to promote sustainable environmental practices as well as reduce poverty in rural areas, Maathai worked tirelessly throughout her life to promote conservationism, as well as to support civil and women's rights organizations and champion democracy in Kenya.

Maathai not only resisted the increasing urbanization of Kenya's crucial natural areas, she worked diligently within her position in the government to advocate for women's rights, but also to stand up against the perception that women deserved no voice in government. Elected to the position of Assistant Minister for Environment, Natural Resources, and Wildlife in 2002 with an astounding 98% of the vote, Maathai used her newfound political power to advocate for the environment and push for conservation education. Despite meeting extreme backlash many times during her political career, Maathai was unflinching, continuing to work for healthier, sustainable ecological practices throughout Kenya both on a macro and micro level, and expanding the Green Belt Movement throughout Africa.

Maathai's resistance came not only in her speeches at conferences internationally, including the United Nations, she also worked closely with women in rural townships to encourage the replanting of many forest areas, and pushed against the Kenyan government to prevent overdevelopment of natural areas in order to support the delicate environmental balance. Outspoken and intelligent, Maathai defied traditional gender roles, speaking out against injustice wherever she visited. The Green Belt Movement works by reaching out to women in small villages as they are the ones in tune with the environmental issues in the area, such as poor water supplies and soil runoff concerns for crops. The movement has been able to bring entire villages into the program, planting over 51 million trees in Kenya and spurring on multiple similar movements around the world.

Maathai cautioned people against becoming overwhelmed by the chaos around them with a metaphor about a hummingbird in a raging forest fire. Even though the forest was burning around the bird, it would still return to the river to bring one droplet of water to the fire to try and quench it. While the effort seemed futile, even that small action made a difference in that area of the forest, and if enough smaller actions inspire people to take up the cause, the effects can be truly spectacular.

YOU
HAVE
SOMETHING
GLORIOUS TO DRAW ON
BEGGING FOR
ATTENTION.
USE IT.

LORRAINE HANSBERRY

"YOU HAVE SOMETHING GLORIOUS TO DRAW ON BEGGING FOR ATTENTION. USE IT."

–Lorraine Hansberry,
"The Nation Needs Your Gifts"
(*Negro Digest*, August 1964)

LORRAINE HANSBERRY

May 19, 1930 to January 12, 1965

Known For: Civil Rights Activism; Anti-Colonialism; LGBTQ Activism; *A Raisin in the Sun* (1959); *The Sign in Sidney Brustein's Window* (1965); *To Be Young, Gifted, and Black* (1969); *Les Blancs* (1970)

Born in Chicago in 1930, Lorraine Hansberry grew up in a household that was often visited by important African American figures such as W.E.B DuBois, Duke Ellington, and Langston Hughes. Her uncle was a scholar of African Studies at Howard University and her father was a civil rights activist and supporter of the National Association for the Advancement of Colored People (NAACP). From a young age, Hansberry was exposed to the harsh reality of living in a segregated America, but through her family she was taught the importance of acting out against injustice. When she was a young child her family bravely relocated to a neighborhood that was restricted to black people. They were met with violence and hatred from a white mob. The Supreme Court of Illinois defended the legality of the neighborhood's restrictions preventing black residents and the family was forced to leave their home. Eventually the decision was reversed and the neighborhoods in that section of Chicago were opened to black families.

After studying visual art as a young adult, Hansberry began her career as a writer. She began writing for a progressive publication called *Freedom*, where she met many like-minded mentors dedicated to protesting racial discrimination. In 1959 her play *A Raisin in the Sun* opened, making her the first black female playwright to be produced on Broadway. Drawing heavily on her personal experiences, the play was highly successful and was named "Best Play" by New York Drama Critics' Circle.

Aside from her successful writing career and work as a civil rights activist, Hansberry was a member of one of the country's first lesbian organizations, Daughters of Bilitis (DOB). She was a writer and thinker who was ahead of her time in many ways, constantly questioning and challenging the status quo. Hansberry tragically died from pancreatic cancer at the age of 34. Her ex-husband and long-time friend Robert Nemiroff became her literary executor and posthumously published three of her unfinished plays, as well as a collection of her other unfinished writing, which he adapted into the stage play *To Be Young, Gifted, and Black* in 1969, which later became a book by the same title (and inspired the Nina Simone song). Hansberry's work within the black community as well as her impact in the LGBTQ community continued well beyond her death, with the DOB surviving until 1995 and her plays paving the way for other black playwrights' works to take their rightful place on the global stage.

UNTIL WE HAVE
THE COURAGE TO
RECOGNIZE CRUELTY
FOR WHAT IT IS—
WHETHER ITS VICTIM IS
HUMAN OR ANIMAL—
WE CANNOT EXPECT
THINGS TO BE MUCH
BETTER IN THIS WORLD

RACHEL CARSON

"UNTIL WE HAVE THE COURAGE TO RECOGNIZE CRUELTY FOR WHAT IT IS—WHETHER ITS VICTIM IS HUMAN OR ANIMAL—WE CANNOT EXPECT THINGS TO BE MUCH BETTER IN THIS WORLD."

–Rachel Carson,
in an undated letter to Fon Boardman

RACHEL CARSON

May 27, 1907 to April 14, 1964

Known For: Environmental Activism; Anti-DDT Activism; Influencing the Creation of the United States Environmental Protection Agency (EPA); *Under the Sea Wind* (1941); *The Sea Around Us* (1951); *Silent Spring* (1962)

Rachel Carson is considered one of the most influential and recognizable environmental activists of the Greatest Generation, her work providing a catalyst for much of the eco-activism of the '60s and '70s. Born in Springdale, Pennsylvania, Carson always knew she wanted to be a writer, publishing her first piece in a national children's magazine when she was 10 years old. Her passion for the written word soon became the primary vehicle for her activism. With a master's degree in zoology, Carson became the second woman hired by the United States Bureau of Fisheries and became the Editor-in-Chief of all publications for the United States Fish and Wildlife Service. Her pieces not only focused on the environment, they also helped show readers their place in the complex tapestry of ecological balance, instead of seeing themselves as outside of the cycle of nature. Even in her early work the push for regulations on the "forces of destruction" facing many natural resources can be seen, a call that would become more pronounced over time.

She focused heavily on sea life in her writings, and published *Under the Sea Wind* in 1941 and *The Sea Around Us* in 1951. She had an innate ability to present biological information in an engaging manner, allowing the average reader to appreciate facts about the natural world without feeling bogged down with information. However, her most impactful book, *Silent Spring*, was published in 1962, inspired by a friend pointing out that there was a noticeable loss of bird life where she lived after the area was sprayed with chemical pesticides. The book made clear the dangers of disrupting the natural world through the use of pesticides like DDT and included information about the dangers to humans, such as the increased risk of developing cancer. While she was largely slandered by the companies manufacturing these chemicals, she managed to reach an audience of around 15 million with her 1963 TV special, "The Silent Spring of Rachel Carson."

Her work was not only corroborated by President John F. Kennedy's Science Advisory Committee Report that same year, but it also helped to put environmental concerns at the forefront of the public discourse and acted as a framework for later books detailing the dangers humans can pose to their environments. Without Carson, the environmental movement may not have come to prominence until much later, and her fortitude in the face of naysayers and those seeking to discredit her is an inspiration for today's environmental activists looking to draw global and political attention to the climate crisis.

DON'T EVER UNDERESTIMATE THE IMPACT YOU CAN HAVE, BECAUSE HISTORY HAS SHOWN US THAT COURAGE CAN BE CONTAGIOUS AND HOPE CAN TAKE ON A LIFE OF ITS OWN.

MICHELLE OBAMA

"DON'T EVER UNDERESTIMATE THE IMPACT YOU CAN HAVE, BECAUSE HISTORY HAS SHOWN US THAT COURAGE CAN BE CONTAGIOUS, AND HOPE CAN TAKE ON A LIFE OF ITS OWN."

–Michelle Obama,
in her keynote address at the Young African Women Leaders Forum (June 22, 2011)

MICHELLE OBAMA

January 17, 1964

Known For: Executive Director for Chicago Chapter of Public Allies; Let's Move! (2010); Reach Higher Initiative (2014); International Girls' Education Support; First Lady of the United States (2009–2017); Co-Founder of Joining Forces (2011); Let Girls Learn (2015); *Becoming* (2018)

Michelle Obama's rise to prominence from the South Side of Chicago is a story of dedication, talent, and commitment. She excelled in school and went on to graduate from Harvard Law School in 1988. Working as a lawyer and public servant long before she became the First Lady of the United States, Obama worked tirelessly not only to increase community involvement but also to help inspire young people to take part in public service. After founding the first community service program at the University of Chicago as Associate Dean of Student Services in 1996, Obama went on to increase volunteerism while working as the Vice President of Community and External Affairs at the University of Chicago Medical Center from 2005 to 2009.

Her work championing young people continued into her tenure as First Lady. In 2010, she launched Let's Move!, a program aimed at ending childhood obesity in one generation. She drew attention to the benefits of organic, healthy eating by starting a vegetable garden on the White House grounds. Obama also worked to encourage students of all backgrounds to strive for higher education with the Reach Higher Initiative, founded to help teach students about financial aid, college and career opportunities, and summer learning opportunities, as well as supporting high school counselors in their efforts to help students get accepted to colleges. Her dedication to education also extended beyond efforts in the United States, helping support international girls' education programs that ensured girls of all ages access to education without threat.

Despite enduring criticism during her time as First Lady, Obama engendered the position with a sense of class as well as compassion that has left its mark not only on the White House but on the world. In her final speech as First Lady on January 13, 2017, she encouraged the youth of America to "lead by example with hope; never fear." She continues to be an inspiration to people from all walks of life and stands as a role model for girls everywhere to speak up for what they believe in and never give up on their education.

WE MAY ENCOUNTER MANY DEFEATS, BUT WE MUST NOT BE DEFEATED.

MAYA ANGELOU

"WE MAY ENCOUNTER MANY DEFEATS, BUT WE MUST NOT BE DEFEATED."

–Maya Angelou,
in her interview with George Plimpton in "The Art of Fiction No. 119" (*The Paris Review*, Issue 116, Fall 1990)

MAYA ANGELOU

April 4, 1928 to May 28, 2014

Known For: Civil Rights Activism; *I Know Why the Caged Bird Sings* (1969); Emmy Award nomination for *Roots* (1977); Contributor to the Organization of African American Unity; Feature Editor of "The African Review"; Inducted into the National Women's Hall of Fame (1998); Recipient of the National Medal of the Arts (2000); Recipient of the Lincoln Medal (2008); Recipient of the Presidential Medal of Freedom (2011)

Born Marguerite Johnson, Maya Angelou spent a portion of her childhood in then-harshly segregated Stamps, Arkansas. Known for her writing, acting, and participation in the Civil Rights Movement, Angelou's accomplishments crossed creative boundaries, adding countless works to the canon of African American literature. Her work as a screenwriter and actress, especially her Emmy-nominated role in the TV miniseries *Roots* (1977), exposed her to larger audiences, making her an internationally recognized figure.

However, her life was far from easy. After being sexually assaulted at the age of 8, Angelou refused to speak for 5 years after her assailant was murdered, as she attributed his death to her speaking out about the crime. In an interview with the *Paris Review* in 1990, Angelou talked about this period in her life: "I loved the black poets, and I loved Shakespeare, and Edgar Allan Poe, and I liked Matthew Arnold a lot—still do. Being mute for a number of years, I read and memorized, and all those people have had tremendous influence." She mentioned that her incredible writing skills were connected to this love of books.

Angelou's memoir, *I Know Why the Caged Bird Sings* (1969) has been praised for its discussion of the lives of African American women, a subject that was largely underrepresented in the popular literature of the time. Angelou dealt with the struggles of her life in unapologetic terms, and, as Hilton Als wrote in *The New Yorker* in 2002, it was one of the first memoirs to write "about blackness from the inside, without apology or defense." For her incredible contributions to both the literary world and her personal activism, Angelou was awarded the Presidential Medal of Freedom in 2011, and her work has laid the foundation for countless women writers to speak their own experience through literature.

THERE SHOULD NEVER BE ANOTHER SEASON OF SILENCE UNTIL WOMAN HAD THE SAME RIGHTS EVERYWHERE ON THIS GREEN EARTH, AS MAN.

EQUALITY

SAFETY

JUSTICE

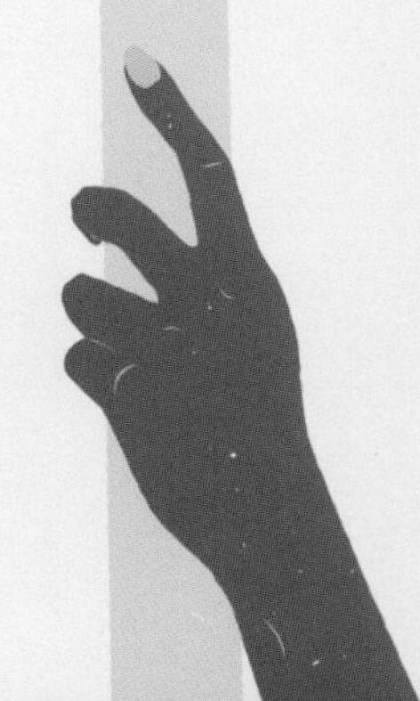

SUSAN B. ANTHONY

"THERE SHOULD NEVER BE ANOTHER SEASON OF SILENCE UNTIL WOMAN HAD THE SAME RIGHTS EVERYWHERE ON THIS GREEN EARTH, AS MAN."

–Susan B. Anthony,
remarking on the Kansas Campaign of 1867

SUSAN B. ANTHONY

February 15, 1820 to March 13, 1906

Known For: Women's Suffrage Movement; Women's Rights Activism; Social Reformation; Abolitionism; Temperance Movement; Equal Rights Activism; Founder of *The Revolution* (1868–1872); 1848 Seneca Falls Convention; Co-Founder of the Women's New York State Temperance Society (1852); Co-Founder of the New York State Woman's Rights Committee (c. 1850s); *To the Women of the Republic* (1864); Co-Founder of the American Equal Rights Association (1866); Co-Founder of the National American Woman Suffrage Association (1969); *History of Woman Suffrage* (1881)

The first woman to appear on American currency, Susan B. Anthony has been credited with the success of women's suffrage, so much so that the 19th Amendment to the Constitution of the United States, which gave white women the right to vote, has been nicknamed the "Susan B. Anthony Amendment." While Anthony did not see women's suffrage in her lifetime (and it took until 1965 for there to be universal suffrage in the United States), her efforts in the name of women's rights acted as a foundation for the feminist movements that would come after her.

Anthony championed the cause of women's suffrage, as well as temperance, the abolition of slavery, and equal rights for all regardless of race or sex. Working in tandem with her close friend, Elizabeth Cady Stanton, Anthony helped found several institutions to promote social and political reform, including the American Equal Rights Association and the National American Woman Suffrage Association. Not just looking for voting rights for women, Anthony campaigned for women's right to own property, and published *The Revolution*, a paper with the express goal of bringing awareness to the cause of women's suffrage.

Anthony and Stanton were introduced at the 1848 Seneca Falls Convention where *The Declaration of Sentiments* was presented to outline the oppression suffered by women and to assert their equality in politics, family, education, and job opportunities. This marked the beginning of Anthony's true involvement in the cause of women's rights. She and Stanton traveled across the country, speaking out against the restrictions placed on women, as well as demanding an end to slavery. Anthony continued to persevere despite hostile resistance, including instances where she was hung in effigy, or encountered angry mobs. Not content with just speaking out for the cause of women's suffrage, Anthony voted illegally in 1872, incurring a $100 fine she never paid. While Anthony never saw women's suffrage in her lifetime, her impact on the movement and her steadfast belief that women were equal to men in all respects solidified the women's rights movement, and her work continues to inspire activists today.

THE GREATEST DANGER TO OUR FUTURE IS APATHY

JANE GOODALL

"THE GREATEST DANGER TO OUR FUTURE IS APATHY."

–Jane Goodall,
"The Power of One" (*Time* magazine, August 26, 2002)

JANE GOODALL

April 3, 1934

Known For: Studying Chimpanzees in Gombe National Park, Tanzania; Conservation Activism; Humanitarian Efforts; Introducing Women to the Field of Primatology; Recipient of the Franklin Burr Award for Contribution to Science (1963–64); Recipient of the National Geographic Society Hubbard Medal for Distinction in Exploration, Discovery, and Research (1995); Recipient of the United Nations Messenger of Peace Appointment (2002); Recipient of the Time Magazine European Heroes Award (2004); Recipient of the United States Department of the Interior Secretary's Lifetime Achievement Award (2009)

Growing up in England, Jane Goodall's interest in animals began thanks to a stuffed chimpanzee named Jubilee that went everywhere with her. Goodall always knew that she wanted to study wildlife. Her dream was to go to Africa to observe animals in the wild and write about them. Her mother encouraged her to follow this dream and use every resource available to her to achieve it. In 1957 on a visit to Kenya, Goodall met paleontologist Dr. Louis S. B. Leakey. Impressed by her knowledge and enthusiasm for animals, Leakey hired Goodall as his assistant. She was only 23 years old at the time, and she had not attended college because she was unable to afford it. Remembering her mother's advice, Goodall recognized the chance to achieve her dream by working with Leakey and she jumped at the opportunity.

In 1960, Leakey and Goodall began studying chimpanzees by Lake Tanganyika. Controlled by the British Government, British authorities were opposed to a young woman like Goodall going there without a companion. Her mother volunteered to leave Britain and accompany her daughter on the trip so that she could continue her work. Goodall then traveled to Gombe Stream Chimpanzee Reserve in Tanzania where she studied and learned from the chimpanzees she observed in the wild. It was here that Goodall made some of the most important discoveries about chimpanzees that scholars have made to date. She observed chimpanzees hunting and eating meat, as well as using sticks to collect and eat termites. These discoveries disproved the widely held beliefs that chimpanzees were vegetarian, and that humans were the only species on earth to create tools.

Her time in Gombe and the discoveries she made there began to attract attention. In 1962, Goodall was accepted to Cambridge University as a PhD candidate despite the fact that she was a woman in a field dominated by men and did not hold a college degree. Goodall refused to let these things hold her back from the work that she knew was her calling. From there, Goodall went on to dedicate the rest of her life to studying chimpanzees and spreading important information on how to protect these animals in the wild and conserve their habitat. Goodall is known for giving the chimpanzees she studies human names rather than numbers, which is part of her larger goal to spread her belief that chimpanzees have complex minds, individual personalities, and emotions.

Today, Goodall continues to educate the public on issues such as habitat destruction and how people play a part in the well-being of wild animals. Through the Roots & Shoots program, the Jane Goodall Institute continues to inspire young people around the globe to get involved in solving problems in their communities.

I WAS BORN A BITCH, I WAS BORN A PAINTER.

FRIDA KAHLO

"I WAS BORN A BITCH, I WAS BORN A PAINTER."

–Frida Kahlo,
in an unsent letter to her husband, Diego Rivera,
as translated in *Finding Frida Kahlo* (2009)

FRIDA KAHLO

July 6, 1907 to July 13, 1954

Known For: Feminist Movement; Anti-Colonialism Activism; Association with the *Mexicanidad* Movement; *Mexicayotl* Movement; *The Two Fridas* (1939); *Self-Portrait with Thorn Necklace and Hummingbird* (1940); *The Broken Column* (1944)

Frida Kahlo's appearance is as instantly recognizable as her paintings, many of which are self-portraits reflecting magical realism and surrealist themes. Kahlo not only embraced Mexican traditions and symbolism in her artwork, she made a point to reject European beauty standards in her personal appearance, embracing the aspects of her look that reflected her heritage. There is a certain strength in choosing the way you present yourself to the world, and Kahlo wielded her appearance like many powerful women who have come both before and after. Choosing to dress in traditional clothing, Kahlo's life became as striking as her own artwork, a brush stroke of defiance against the colonial pressures surrounding her life.

Through her self-portraits, Kahlo explored aspects of herself and the world around her in abstract terms, and the symbolism worked into her imagery belied her own struggles with social norms, femininity, machoism, and the concept of taboo. Physically unwell through most of her life, Kahlo's artwork represented the deep ache of self-loathing, the complexities of chronic pain, and the layers that come with personal identity. Her striking expressions of her inner self have become synonymous with women's freedom. Through the multifaceted lens of her own body as subject, Kahlo represented societal conflict in a granular, personal way, placing issues like motherhood and the threat of the patriarchy in the open for viewers to wrestle with. Embracing the *Mexicanidad* movement, which sought to remove the stigma presenting Mexican culture as "inferior" to European and American cultures, Kahlo not only represented her background with her artwork, but allowed it to become a large part of her identity.

Involved in the Communist Party through her tumultuous marriage to painter Diego Rivera, Kahlo and Rivera often represented their political beliefs in their works, such as Rivera including Soviet leader Vladimir Lenin in a mural commissioned by Nelson Rockefeller for the Rockefeller Center. This portion was painted over by Rockefeller, but the message remained, arguably heightened by the censorship.

Her art was not only an outlet for her own personal turmoil within her marriage and her physical body, it represented the struggle of her nation as it fought to preserve its cultural identity as it experienced political upheaval. Through her artwork and her life, Kahlo worked to advance the position of women in society and take back her own power from those trying to erase her identity, asserting her proud defiance and creativity.

MARSHA P. JOHNSON

"PAY IT NO MIND."

–Marsha P. Johnson's
answer when a judge asked her what her middle initial referenced

---

MARSHA P. JOHNSON

August 24, 1945 to July 6, 1992

Known For: LGBTQ Rights Activism; The Stonewall Riots (1969); Transgender Rights Activism; Founder of Street Transgender Action Revolutionaries (STAR); ACT UP and AIDS Activism Work

Marsha "Pay It No Mind" Johnson was one of the central figures of the gay rights movement throughout the '60s and '70s. Living her life as a drag queen on the streets of New York City, Johnson was known for her colorful outfits and her infectious friendliness. While Johnson may be best recognized as a member of the Stonewall Riots in 1969, the spark that ignited the gay pride movement and helped bring public awareness to the LGBTQ community, her impact extended far beyond her participation at the riot. Johnson acted as a supporter for all of New York's homeless gay and transgender individuals and was known to give away the money she had to those who needed it more than she did. For those who lived in Greenwich Village, Johnson became a symbol of more than just flamboyance. She was dubbed a saint of the gay community thanks to her activism and participation in gay rights parades, as well as her impact in co-founding Street Transvestite (now Transgender) Action Revolutionaries, a group dedicated to help gay and transgender individuals kicked out of their homes.

While Johnson has been applauded for defying gender stereotypes and restrictions and working tirelessly for the gay community, one of the most memorable aspects of her personality was that she was not trying to conform to anyone's perceptions of herself or how she should appear. With outfits made from thrift store items and hairpieces of flowers, she embraced her true identity and put it on display for those around her. Although there is shaky evidence that Johnson herself was the one who began the police confrontation at the Stonewall Riots, her daily confrontation with the challenges of living on the street as a drag queen and a gender-nonconforming individual was immensely impactful to the neighborhood around her, and her legacy has gone on to inspire countless members of the LGBTQ community to embrace their identities with pride. When Johnson was found dead under mysterious circumstances in 1992, her funeral drew hundreds of mourners, and the New York City police allowed the mourners to close down the streets so they could give her one last sendoff as a testament to her spirit, individuality, and her tenacity to tell the world, "Pay it no mind."

ONE CHILD,
ONE TEACHER,
ONE BOOK,
AND ONE PEN
CAN CHANGE
THE WORLD

MALALA YOUSAFZAI

"ONE CHILD, ONE TEACHER, ONE BOOK, AND ONE PEN CAN CHANGE THE WORLD."

–Malala Yousafzai,
in her speech at the United Nations (July 12, 2013)

MALALA YOUSAFZAI

July 12, 1997

Known For: Education Activism; Women's Rights Activism; Activist for Peace; Recipient of the Pakistan National Youth Peace Prize (2011); International Children's Peace Prize (2011); Recipient of the Sakharov Prize for Freedom of Thought (2013); Joint Recipient of the Nobel Peace Prize (2014); Founder of the Malala Fund

Life for Malala Yousafzai changed rapidly after the Taliban, a radical militant Islamic group, gained control of the Swat Valley in Pakistan in 2007. Under the Taliban's rule, social activities such as dancing and watching TV were banned, as well as any form of education for girls. In just one year, the Taliban destroyed approximately 400 schools. Despite the constant threat of suicide bombers and militants, Yousafzai continued to go to school, and pushed back against the violent oppostion to girls' education. Even after being forced to leave her home by the approaching war between Pakistan and the Taliban, both Yousafzai and her father, Ziauddin, continued to push for safe, free education for girls, using the media to broadcast their message, despite the threat it posed to their own safety. Yousafzai was nominated for the International Children's Peace Prize and awarded the Pakistan National Youth Peace Prize for her work in education in 2011. However, her outcry against the Taliban had gained attention, and on October 9, 2012, Yousafzai was shot three times by a member of the Taliban while on a bus heading home from school. Despite the seriousness of her wounds and multiple corrective surgeries, Yousafzai recovered and continues to push for education access for girls around the world. She was the joint recipient of the Nobel Peace Prize in 2014, making her the youngest person to be honored by this award.

Yousafzai continues to prioritize education, both for herself and others, working to support education for girls in Kenya and Nigeria, as well as other refugees of war. She and her father founded the Malala Fund in 2014, an organization that invests in local education activists, works to hold local leaders accountable for their roles in education, and provides a platform for girls to share their stories. Yousafzai is now studying philosophy, politics, and economics at the University of Oxford, but her efforts to ensure all girls are given access to free, high-quality education have not stopped.

THE STAKES ARE TOO HIGH TO DWELL ON WHAT MIGHT HAVE BEEN. WE HAVE TO WORK TOGETHER FOR WHAT STILL CAN BE.

HILLARY RODHAM CLINTON

"THE STAKES ARE TOO HIGH TO DWELL ON WHAT MIGHT HAVE BEEN. WE HAVE TO WORK TOGETHER FOR WHAT STILL CAN BE."

–Hillary Rodham Clinton,
in her presidential candidate nomination concession speech (June 7, 2008)

HILLARY RODHAM CLINTON

October 26, 1947

Known For: First Lady of the United States (1993–2001); United States Senator (2001–2009); Task Force on National Healthcare; United States Secretary of State (2009–2013); First Female Presidential Candidate Nominated by a Major Party (2016); Children's Rights Advocacy; Women's Rights Advocacy

Born in Chicago, Illinois, Hillary Rodham Clinton's lifetime achievements alone stand as a testament to the power of women in political and professional fields. As a law school graduate, Clinton worked alongside the Children's Defense Fund (CDF) to ensure a level playing field for all children, and to help provide education, opportunities, and protection to children from all backgrounds. She served as a member of the board at CDF from 1986 to 1989 and helped to found the Arkansas Advocates for Children and Families in 1977. Her passion for helping marginalized groups find their voice continued well into her tenure as First Lady of the United States, when she advocated for women's rights, children's issues, and healthcare reform on a national level. Yet, for all of her positive work as First Lady there were those who attacked her for holding her own views separate from her husband and framed her stance that she would rather be on the field making a difference instead of staying home and baking as an attack on traditional women's roles.

Not allowing the pressure and slander of the media and her opponents to slow her down, Clinton was elected to represent New York State in the United States Senate, a position she held until her appointment as Secretary of State by President Barack Obama in 2008. During her time as senator, Clinton fought for increased access to health care and education, investment in alternate energy resources, and to modernize schools. Her work toward the betterment of others and her commitment to extending resources to all continued through her term as Secretary of State and 2016 presidential campaign, where she became the first female presidential candidate nominated by a major party. While Clinton did not win the presidency, she did win a majority of the national vote, surpassing her competitor by 3 million votes and illustrating that women belong in every branch of government.

BECOME SO SKILLED, SO VIGILANT, SO FLAT OUT FANTASTIC AT WHAT YOU DO THAT YOUR TALENT CANNOT BE DISMISSED.

OPRAH WINFREY

"BECOME SO SKILLED, SO VIGILANT, SO FLAT OUT FANTASTIC AT WHAT YOU DO THAT YOUR TALENT CANNOT BE DISMISSED."

–Oprah Winfrey,
in her commencement speech at USC Annenberg School for Communication and Journalism (May 11, 2018)

OPRAH WINFREY

January 29, 1954

Known For: Education Access Supporter; AIDS Activism; Host of *The Oprah Winfrey Show* (1986–2011); Founder of the Oprah Winfrey Scholars Program (1989); Sponsorship of the National Child Protection Act (1993); Founder of Oprah's Angel Network (1998); Founder of *O, The Oprah Magazine* (2000); The Oprah Winfrey Foundation (2002); Founder of the Oprah Winfrey Leadership Academy for Girls (2007)

Oprah Winfrey has become one of the most identifiable influencers of the 21st century, with a list of properties, TV shows, and charitable organizations that exceeds comprehension. Beginning her career as a TV personality at the Nashville television station WTVF-TV at the age of 19, Winfrey found herself stifled by the objectivity and constraint required by a news reporter, finding her stride in a casual talk show format instead with her co-host position on a local talk show. Winfrey's popularity soared when she became the host of the then-faltering *AM Chicago* talk show in 1984. Thanks to her involvement, the ratings soared, and the program was renamed *The Oprah Winfrey Show*. It earned several Emmy Awards, and became one of the highest-rated talk shows in the United States. Winfrey's popularity and influence over consumers and the general public has been called "The Oprah Effect," and impacts everything from diet trends, media consumption, political leanings, and book reception, with any books featured by Winfrey being guaranteed at least 1 million additional book sales. The format of her talk show has also given rise to the concept of "Oprahfication," referring to public confession in the form of interviews as a type of therapy. Her openness about her own struggles and her willingness to display an emotional response to a topic during her interviews have helped create an openness around many subjects otherwise considered taboo by the American public.

Winfrey's popularity has only increased her charity work, with her being listed as one of the most generous Americans, donating over $400 million to educational causes by 2012. She not only founded the Oprah's Angel Network to help fund charitable causes and human rights organizations, she has participated in several South African outreach programs, including donation efforts for children with AIDS and founding The Oprah Winfrey Leadership Academy for Girls in 2007. Much of her charity work focuses on improving the lives and safety of children, and with her support the National Child Protection Act, colloquially known as the "Oprah Bill," was signed into law in 1993. She continues to support charitable organizations around the world and uses her influence to help inspire others to work for change in their society.

NEVER LET GO OF THAT FIERY SADNESS CALLED DESIRE

PATTI SMITH

"NEVER LET GO OF THAT FIERY SADNESS CALLED DESIRE."

–Patti Smith,
Babel (1978)

PATTI SMITH

December 30, 1946

Known For: Poet Laureate of Punk; Punk Rock Movement; Human Rights Activism; *Horses* (1975); "Gloria" (1975); Recipient of the Académie Charles Cros Grand Prix du Disque Award (1975); "Because the Night" (1978); "People Have the Power" (1988); Recipient of the Women of Valor Award (2005); Commandeur de l'Ordre des Arts et des Lettres (2005); *Just Kids* (2010)

Known as the "Poet Laureate of Punk," Patti Smith's songs combine the attitude now synonymous with the punk movement and the gravely quality of garage-rock music for a raw, emotional sound. When Smith released her first album, *Horses,* in 1975, rock 'n' roll was overwhelmed by the arena-rock scene, which focused on studio-polished performances. Smith's work trended toward the experimental, truly original soundscape that rock was first known for, upending the retouched and pitch-perfect recordings popular at the time. It wasn't just her sound that grabbed people's attention, it was the power of her lyrics, which ranged from heretical in her quasi-cover of the 1965 *Them* song "Gloria" to the disturbing imagery that flowed as a through line in *Horses*. As she told *Filler Magazine* in 2008, "I wanted to remember the original energy; strip away all the glamour and limousines and tons of drugs. I wanted to get back to the revolutionary ideas, merging poetry and rhythm and rock and roll."

In the late '70s, Smith left the city that shaped her (as masterfully documented in her memoir *Just Kids*, which focuses on her time living with photographer Robert Mapplethorpe) and moved to Detroit and announced her retirement. But in August 1993, an appearance at Central Park SummerStage marked her triumphant return to both New York and performing. And since then her creative output has been nothing short of prolific, from albums to books of poetry and prose, as well as activism.

From her criticism of the Iraq War to her involvement with AIDS/HIV awareness and the Green Party, Smith has never sacrificed personal or artistic integrity and has always spoken up for what she believes in, living up to the powerfully unifying message of her 1988 song "People Have the Power."

WE ALL HAVE THE POWER TO NAME OURSELVES

GLORIA STEINEM

"WE ALL HAVE THE POWER TO NAME OURSELVES."

–Gloria Steinem,
in an interview with *The Humanist* (June 7, 2012)

GLORIA STEINEM

March 25, 1934

Known For: Feminist Movement; Women's Rights Activism; Anti-Vietnam War Activism; Civil Rights Activism; Equal Rights Amendment Campaign; Reproductive Rights Movement; Founder of *Ms.* Magazine (1971); Founder of the National Women's Political Caucus (1971); Founder of the Ms. Foundation for Women (1972); Founder of the United States Women's Media Center (2005); Recipient of the Presidential Medal of Freedom (2013)

When talking about the feminist movement, you'd be hard-pressed to find a more recognizable figure than Gloria Steinem. Her influence on the movement as a whole has been far-reaching and comprehensive, bolstering the fight for women's equality, reproductive rights, and more with her powerful command of the English language and forceful personality. A supporter of the Equal Rights Amendment, Steinem has been speaking out against women's oppression for decades, as well as supporting Civil Rights initiatives and participating in the Anti-Vietnam War protests of the late '60s. She is the author of many books on activism, women's rights, and the issues facing women in societies around the world.

Her work is an incredible example of the impact one person can have across multiple causes: from the founding of the National Women's Political Caucus to support women's political involvement both in voting and leading capacities, to co-founding *Ms.* magazine, which provides a platform for feminist discussions and women writers to speak out about issues like personal freedom, body autonomy, and to raise awareness about women's rights in other countries. Steinem's work hones in on the ground-level changes that can be made within individual mindsets to help change the way society views itself, and to give women the tools they need to speak out and stand up for themselves.

Long before her career as a journalist began, Steinem witnessed the discrimination against her mother, who was unable to find employment in middle age due to being a mother, and who continually had her mental illness and struggles downplayed by doctors due to her gender. Steinem notes that both these instances helped her understand the inequality faced by women on a daily basis, a stance that only grew as her journalism and activism careers developed. Steinem used her journalism to cover topics close to the women's rights movement, including the stigma surrounding women who have had abortions, a cause that Steinem noted was the impetus for her entrance into the field of activism.

Her activism not only works to help lift women up, it allows them to define their own identity using the terms they have chosen or reclaimed, giving them a sense of purpose within the movement and helping overthrow the dim view many hold toward outspoken women.

Steinem serves as an empowering figure for women of all ages, proving that social justice and activism are not just for one age group or one generation. And with her ongoing involvement in political and social activism only growing over the years, Steinem has more than proven her own assertation that "Women may be the one group that grows more radical with age."